GETTING TO KNOW
THE U.S. PRESIDENTS

WILLIAM HOWARD
TAFT

TWENTY-SEVENTH PRESIDENT
1909 – 1913

WRITTEN AND ILLUSTRATED BY MIKE VENEZIA

CHILDREN'S PRESS®
A DIVISION OF SCHOLASTIC INC.
NEW YORK   TORONTO   LONDON   AUCKLAND   SYDNEY
MEXICO CITY   NEW DELHI   HONG KONG
DANBURY, CONNECTICUT

Reading Consultant: Nanci R. Vargus, Ed.D., Assistant Professor, School of Education, University of Indianapolis

Historical Consultant: Marc J. Selverstone, Ph.D., Assistant Professor, Miller Center of Public Affairs, University of Virginia

Photographs © 2007: Art Resource, NY/Lewis Wickes Hine/Snark: 29; Corbis Images: 6, 22 (Bettmann), 27 (W.Perry Conway), 21, 25; Library of Congress: 28 (Lewis Hine), 24, 26; Mary Evans Picture Library/ET Compton: 17; Superstock, Inc.: 3; The Art Archive/Picture Desk: 32 (Culver Pictures), 16 (Laurie Platt Winfrey); William Howard Taft National Historic Site: 9, 12, 20.

Colorist for illustrations: Andrew Day

Library of Congress Cataloging-in-Publication Data

Venezia, Mike.
  William Howard Taft / written and illustrated by Mike Venezia.
      p. cm. — (Getting to know the U.S. presidents)
  ISBN-10: 0-516-22631-2 (lib. bdg.)   0-516-25239-9 (pbk.)
  ISBN-13: 978-0-516-22631-6 (lib. bdg.) 978-0-516-25239-1 (pbk.)
  1. Taft, William H. (William Howard), 1857-1930—Juvenile literature. 2.
Presidents—United States—Biography—Juvenile literature. I. Title.
  E762.V46 2006
  973.91'2092-dc22   2006000460

1 2 3 4 5 6 7 8 9 10 R 16 15 14 13 12 11 10 09 08 07

A portrait of William Howard Taft by Anders Leonard Zorn

William Howard Taft was the twenty-seventh president of the United States. He was born in Cincinnati, Ohio, in 1857. William Taft never really wanted to be president. He was much more interested in serving his country as a judge on the United States Supreme Court. After he was president, William's dream finally came true. In 1921, he became chief justice of the Supreme Court.

The United States government is made up
of three sections, or branches. The president
is the leader of the executive branch. The
Supreme Court is the highest court of the
judicial branch. It has nine justices, including
its leader, the chief justice. Congress, the
lawmaking branch, is made up of senators
and representatives. William Taft was the only

TAF'T STRESS CHART

SO-SO

SOMEWHAT
RELAXED AND HAPPY

TOTALLY
RELAXED AND HAPPY

man in U.S. history to hold the top job in two
of the three branches of U.S. government.
William Taft was also the only president who
weighed over 300 pounds. William gained
or lost weight according to how much stress
he was going through. People could almost
tell how happy or upset William was by how
much he weighed.

William Taft came from a pretty wealthy family. His father was a well-respected lawyer. He became the secretary of war and attorney general under President Ulysses S. Grant. He was also a U.S. ambassador.

William Taft was born in this house in Cincinnati, Ohio.

While growing up, Willie Taft and his friends had some run-ins with jealous kids from poorer neighborhoods. Willie always tried to solve problems before they turned into fights. But sometimes he and his friends were forced into stone-throwing wars. Because Willie Taft was always the biggest kid in the group, his friends were glad to have him around when there was trouble.

William Taft's weight problems started when he was a young boy. Willie was often nervous about pleasing his demanding parents. He would overeat to relieve his worries.

William Taft (middle person in bottom row) in high school

Mr. and Mrs. Taft were loving parents, but insisted their children excel in everything they did, especially when it came to school grades. Willie never disappointed his parents. He graduated at the top of his class in high school, and second in his class when he graduated from Yale University.

After studying at Yale, William decided to become a lawyer like his father. He then went to the University of Cincinnati Law School. William also worked part-time reporting court cases for a local newspaper.

Mr. Taft was proud of his son, but began to worry after William finished law school. William didn't seem to be interested in becoming a lawyer right away. Instead, he decided to keep working as a court reporter.

William also started to enjoy himself by going out on dates and to parties. William Taft was very popular and fun to be around. Even though he was large, he was light on his feet and an excellent dancer.

Being a court reporter turned out to be a good job for William. He could see just how the court system worked and how the courts could be improved. Eventually, William got more serious about his law career.

Just before he had graduated from law school, William met a girl he really liked. Her name was Helen Herron.

William Taft (center) and Nellie Herron (seated at left) at a book club gathering

Helen, whose nickname was Nellie, was very smart and energetic. She started a book club, and had gatherings at her home that William often attended.

After six years of dating, William and Nellie got married. Nellie was responsible for encouraging, and sometimes even insisting, that her husband try for bigger and better jobs throughout his life.

Nellie Taft had always dreamed of living in the White House and being the first lady of the United States. She thought the best way to get there was for William to run for elected positions and get appointed to political jobs.

Over the years, William Taft was appointed to a number of jobs in the court system. He was an assistant prosecutor, a judge in the Cincinnati Superior Court, and a U.S. circuit judge.

These jobs earned William lots of respect. He hoped his reputation as a fair and wise judge would help him become a U.S. Supreme Court justice someday.

A painting showing a battle in the Philippines during the Spanish-American War

In 1900, William Taft received a request to meet with President McKinley. William thought he might be offered a job in the Supreme Court. But President McKinley had something else in mind for William. When the United States won the Spanish-American War in 1898, it had gained control of the Philippine Islands. McKinley wanted William to go to the Philippines and help set up a new government there.

William Taft's job would be to head a group that would set up a constitution, create new laws, and appoint or elect government officials. At first, William wasn't sure this would be the best thing for him to do. But Nellie thought it was a great idea.

A village scene in the Philippines in the late 1890s

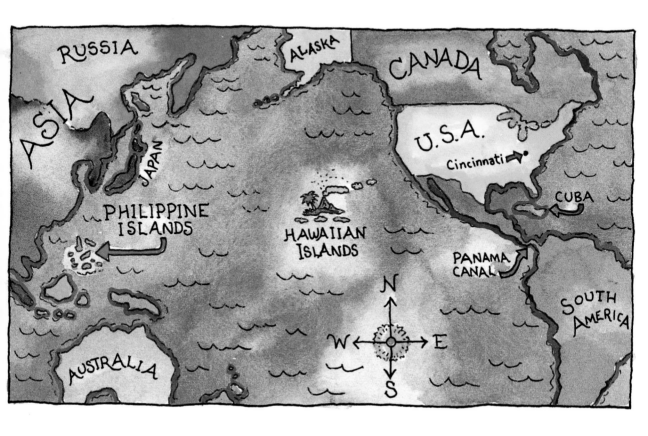

William, Nellie, and their three young
children traveled to the Philippine Islands in
April 1900. It was the beginning of a great
adventure for the Taft family. The islands were
far across the Pacific Ocean, thousands of miles
from their home in Cincinnati.

William was very successful in his new job.
He helped end an armed rebellion and brought

law and order to the country. The Filipino
people loved and trusted the big, jolly William
Taft. He made sure Filipinos took part in
the new government and were involved in
important decisions. William often spent
weeks traveling around the islands to learn
more about the customs and needs of the
Filipino people.

William Taft in the Philippines with his wife and son Charles

While William Taft was in the Philippines, Teddy Roosevelt became president. Teddy had always liked William Taft. He saw what a great job William was doing to help a needy country set up their government. William Taft made sure schools, roads, bridges, and health-care facilities were built.

President Theodore Roosevelt (at head of table, right) with his cabinet, including Secretary of War William Howard Taft (top row, second from right)

President Roosevelt knew a leader like William Taft could help him run the United States. He offered William the job of U.S. secretary of war. William accepted the job. In 1904, he moved his family from the Philippine Islands to Washington, D.C.

William Taft walking along a railroad line during an inspection of the construction of the Panama Canal

As secretary of war, a busy William Taft traveled all over the world, solving one problem after another. He worked on a treaty that ended a war between Russia and Japan. He then helped end a rebellion in Cuba. William even found time to supervise the building of the Panama Canal.

Because William was doing such a great job, President Roosevelt encouraged him to run for president in the next election. Nellie was thrilled. She and Teddy Roosevelt did everything they could to convince William to run for president of the United States.

A political cartoon showing presidential candidate William Taft as a possible crowned "prince," sitting on the shoulders of the "king," Theodore Roosevelt

Teddy Roosevelt had promised not to run for president after his second term ended. Teddy belonged to the Republican Party and was one of the most popular presidents ever. Many Republican Party members were willing to support whomever Teddy recommended to be the next president. Teddy was confident that William Taft would continue to carry out Roosevelt's exciting plans and ideas.

President Taft's inaugural parade on March 4, 1909

When William Taft finally agreed to run for president, Teddy Roosevelt and Nellie Taft were as happy as could be. With Roosevelt's support, William Taft beat the Democratic nominee, William Jennings Bryan. In 1909, William Taft became president of the United States.

William Taft agreed with many of Teddy Roosevelt's policies. He continued to make sure large, powerful companies, called trusts, were controlled. He used the law to stop giant corporations from setting prices too high and forcing smaller companies out of business.

He also worked hard to make it easier for the United States to trade goods and products with Canada and many South American countries.

President Taft continued President Roosevelt's work in breaking apart large, powerful groups of companies called trusts. This political cartoon from the early 1900s shows Uncle Sam using a bright light to "expose" the unfair practices of trusts.

President Taft worked to preserve wilderness areas in the United States.

Like Teddy Roosevelt, President Taft believed in conservation. He supported laws to preserve beautiful wilderness lands. He went against Roosevelt's conservation program, however, by allowing coal-mining companies to use some public lands.

As this photograph by Lewis Hine shows, men, women, and children worked in dark, crowded U.S. factories in the early 1900s.

During the time William Taft was president, millions of immigrants from Europe came to the United States, hoping to find a better life. These people were often forced to work long hours in hot, crowded factories for very little pay. Small children often worked right alongside adults.

This Lewis Hine photo shows young boys working in a U.S. mine in the early 1900s.

President Taft was always concerned about the well being of workers. Just before he left office, President Taft signed a bill that established the Department of Labor. This organization helped to improve workplace conditions and the safety of all workers.

Taft's years as president may have been the unhappiest of his life. He became grouchy and weighed almost 350 pounds. William was so big he once got stuck in his bathtub! Nellie had a special giant tub installed in the White House so her husband would never get stuck again.

Unfortunately, compared to Teddy Roosevelt, people thought William Taft was a pretty dull president. He wasn't very decisive. Sometimes he missed out on important opportunities by taking too much time to think things over.

Over time, Teddy Roosevelt became very disappointed with President Taft. He and other people had thought Taft was going to make big changes in government, but over time, Taft became less willing to do this. During the election of 1912, Teddy decided to come out of retirement and run against his old friend. While Teddy and William were fighting it out, the Democratic candidate, Woodrow Wilson, easily won the election.

A photograph of Chief Justice
William Howard Taft in 1925

William Taft was relieved and happy when his four-year term ended in 1913. His cheery mood returned right away. William began a new job as a law professor at Yale University. He became even happier when he was appointed chief justice of the United States Supreme Court in 1921. Shortly before William Taft died in 1930, he told people he hardly remembered ever being president of the United States.

9582